VISUAL FINANCE

NICHOLAS NIELSEN

Copyright © 2022 by Nic A. Nielsen, CFP®.

All rights reserved. No part of this publication may be reproduced, distributed, or transmitted in any form or by any means, electronic or mechanical, including photocopying, recording, or via any other storage and retrieval system, without prior written permission of the publisher.

Published in the United States by Nic A. Nielsen, CFP®.

Title: Visual Finance

ISBN: 979-8-218-00223-7

Cover Design: Carley Beyer

INTRODUCTION AND ACKNOWLEDGEMENTS

When I first received my securities licenses, I was blessed to partner with two exceptional financial advisors: Chris Barber and John Cooper.

Quickly, I realized the importance of being a great storyteller to help as many families as possible reach financial independence.

Both gentlemen had the incredible ability to illustrate their stories during meetings. I fell in love with this practice and have been honing my sketches ever since.

This book is an attempt to share my favorite sketches that I feel have helped families take the simple next step to improving their financial situation.

You will notice that the following pages contain forty of my sketches, but there is no corresponding text.

In lieu of text, I have created short videos describing what these sketches mean and how they might be applied to your situation.

You may find that many of these sketches are inspired by the works of both Nick Murray and Carl Richards.

In closing, I want to thank my late grandfather Donald Robbins, who encouraged me to learn how money worked so that I could help others and in turn help my family.

I have been blessed to have incredible parents Arthur and Dessa Nielsen, both retired teachers, who have instilled in me a love of learning and the heart of an educator.

Finally, I would like to thank my wife, Jessi, and our children for their support.

Simply scan the QR Code in the bottom right corner of every page that will take you to the corresponding video to get started.

I hope that this is the best book that you will never read!

3 Barbarians Attacking Your Castle

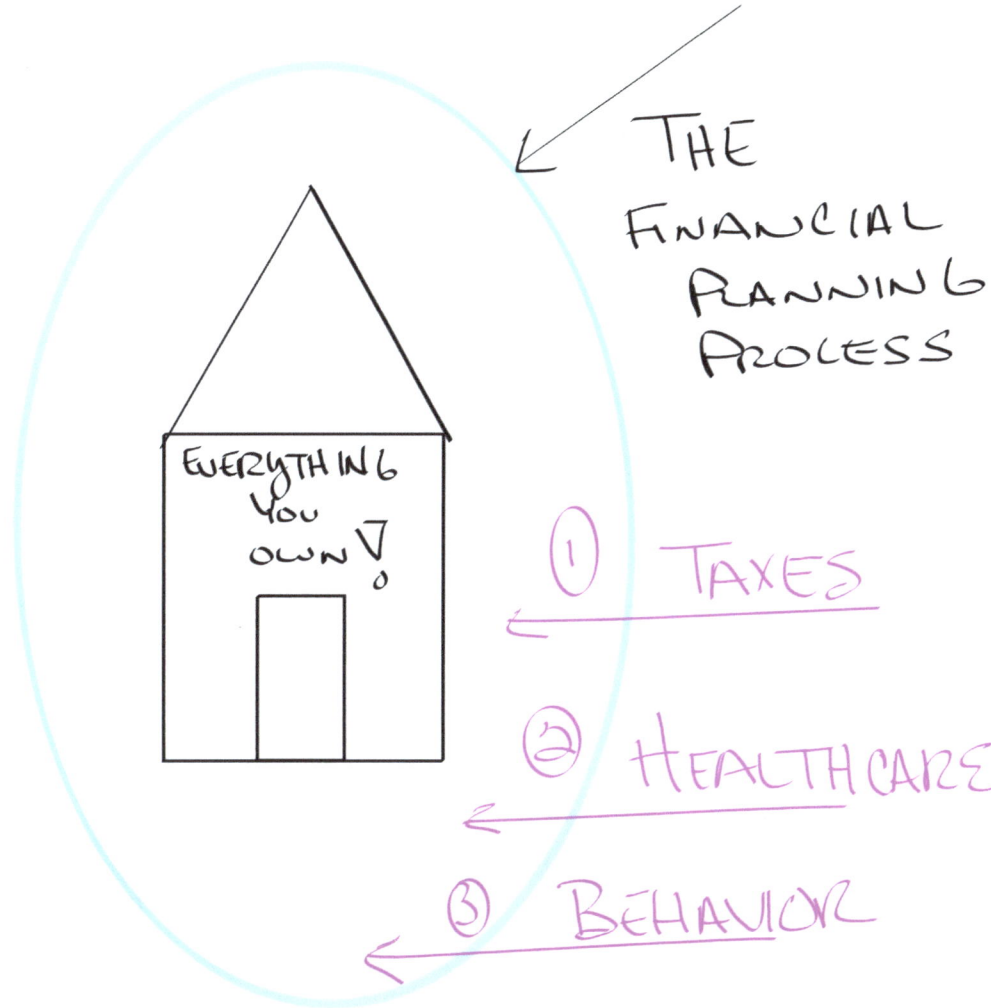

THE FINANCIAL PLANNING PROCESS

EVERYTHING YOU OWN

① TAXES

② HEALTHCARE

③ BEHAVIOR

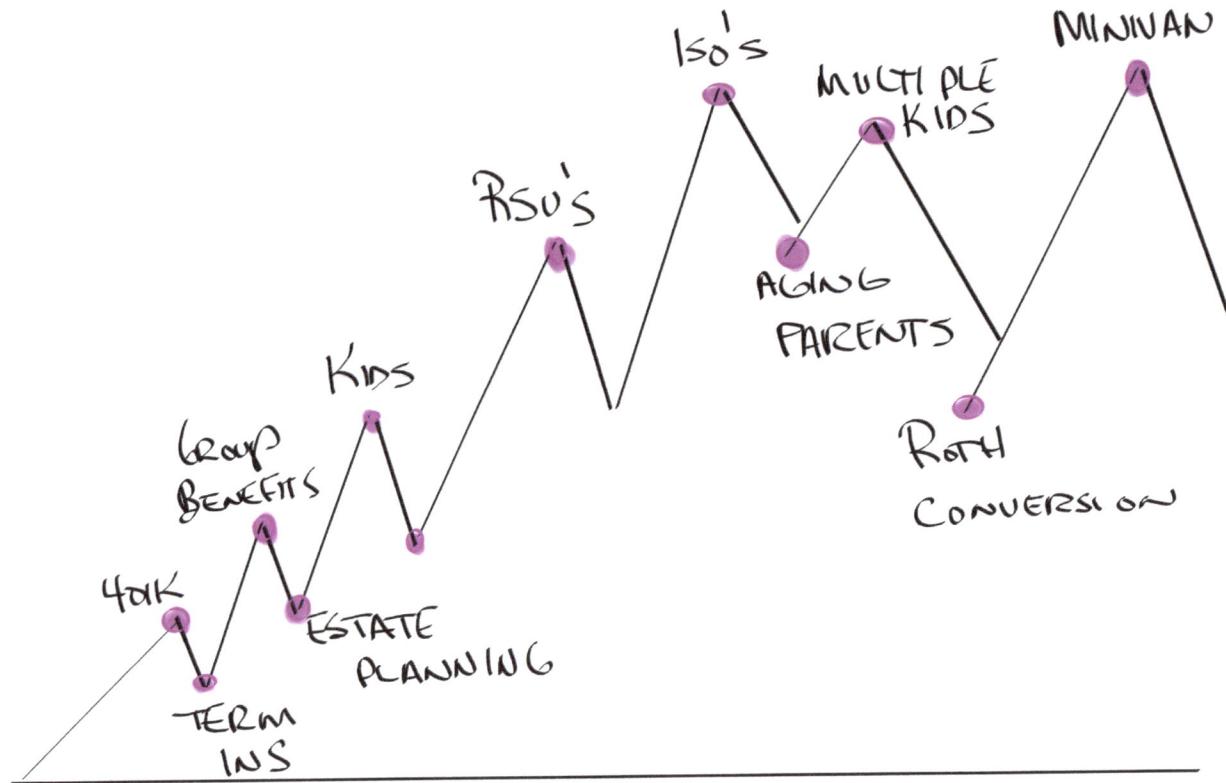

CLIMBING THE COMPLEXITY MOUNTAIN
... NEED A SHERPA?

4 Pulleys Of Financial Independence

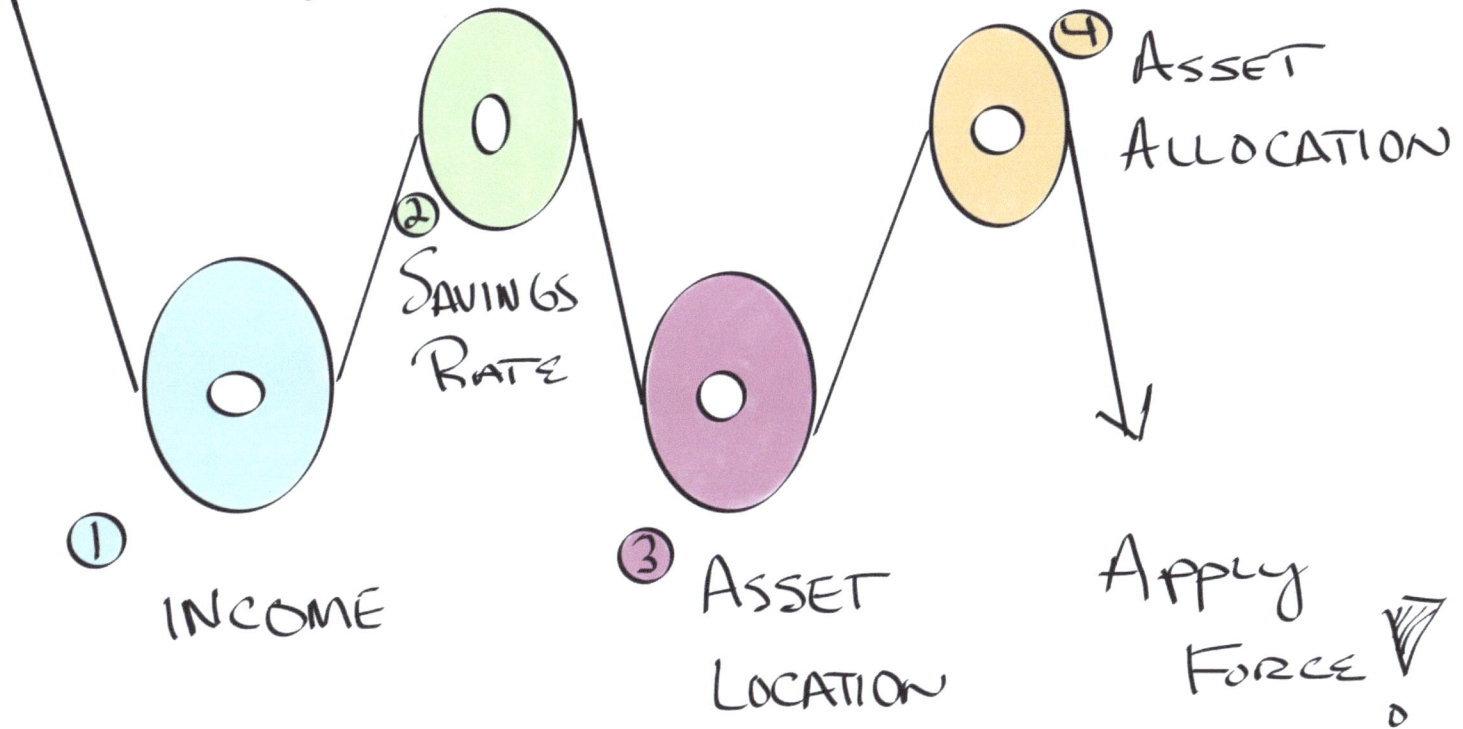

① INCOME

② SAVINGS RATE

③ ASSET LOCATION

④ ASSET ALLOCATION

APPLY FORCE

$$\frac{N_{ic}^{\emptyset}}{S}$$

Cost of Admission

Since WWII, the S&P 500 has...

1. Had Intra Year Declines ≈ 15% ↓
2. Had ≈ 40% Declines ↓ Every 5 yrs
3. Avg ≈ 10% Annual Return ↑ with
   6% Dividend Growth Rate ↑

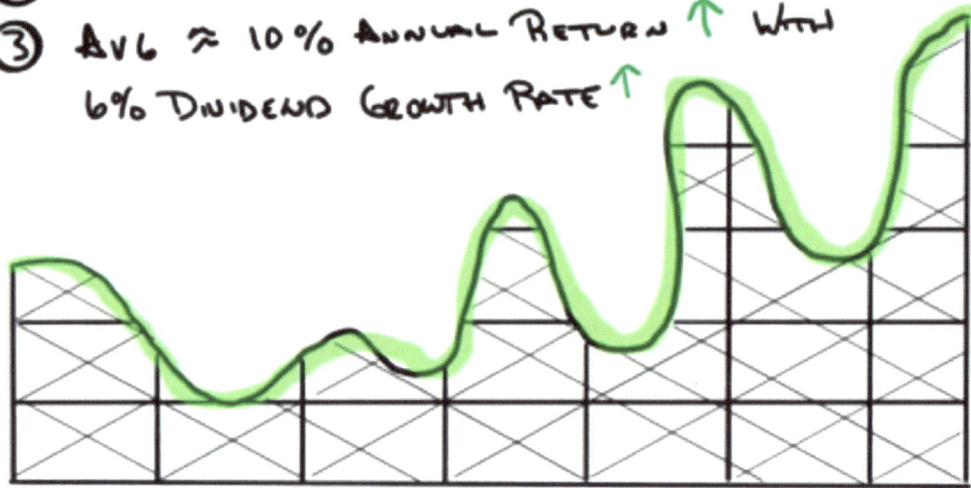

Asset Allocation & Asset Location

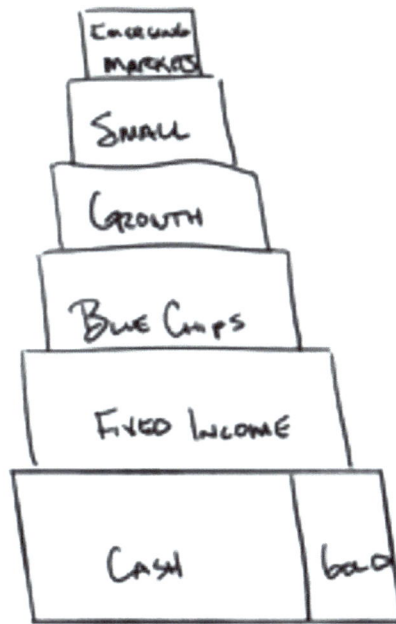

Tax Free

Tax Deferred

Taxable

Nic

If Each Has $2M, Who Has More $?

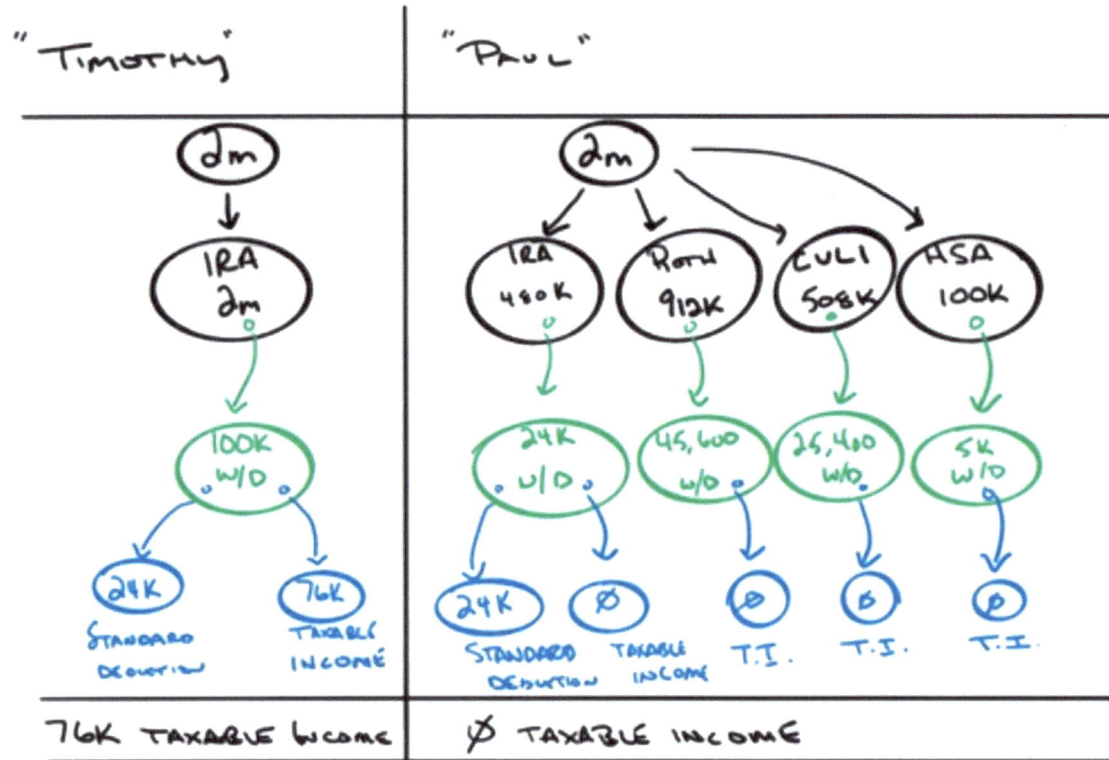

"Timothy"

- 2m → IRA 2m → 100K W/D
  - → 24K — STANDARD DEDUCTION
  - → 76K — TAXABLE INCOME

76K TAXABLE INCOME

"Paul"

- 2m →
  - IRA 480K → 24K W/D → 24K (STANDARD DEDUCTION) → Ø (TAXABLE INCOME)
  - Roth 912K → 45,600 W/D → Ø T.I.
  - CULI 508K → 25,400 W/D → Ø T.I.
  - HSA 100K → 5K W/D → Ø T.I.

Ø TAXABLE INCOME

SURVIVAL OF THE YOUNG EXECUTIVE

THE BIG DROP IS COMING...

What Is $1m?

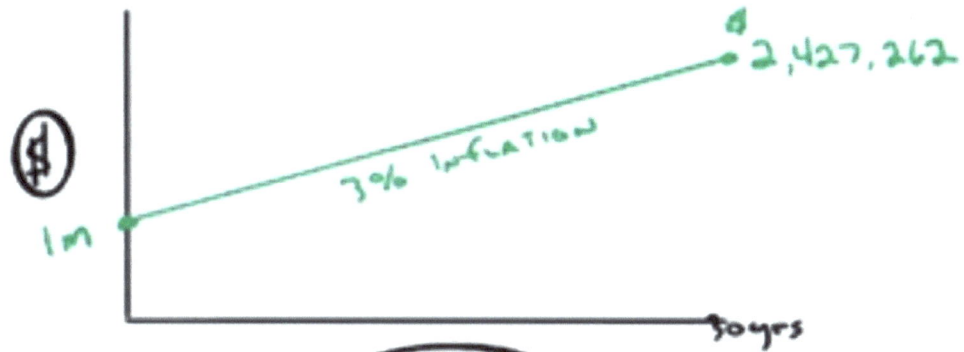

$ $2,427,262$

3% Inflation

$1m

30 yrs

Time

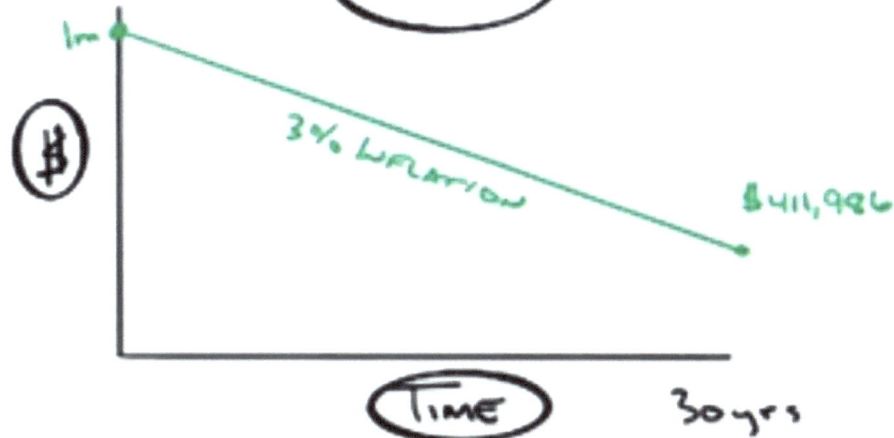

$1m

3% Inflation

$411,986

Time   30 yrs

$$\frac{N_{IC}^{\varnothing}}{2}$$

FINANCIAL STRATEGY CHECKLIST

1. I KNOW WHAT I OWN

2. I KNOW WHY I OWN IT

3. I KNOW WHERE IT FITS INTO MY FINANCIAL PICTURE

4. I UNDERSTAND IN "BOOMS" I WILL UNDERPERFORM

5. I BELIEVE I HAVE A STRATEGY I CAN STICK WITH REGARDLESS OF NEWS HEADLINES OR POLITICAL EVENTS

PERSPECTIVE

DID I GAIN $150K OR LOSE 50K?

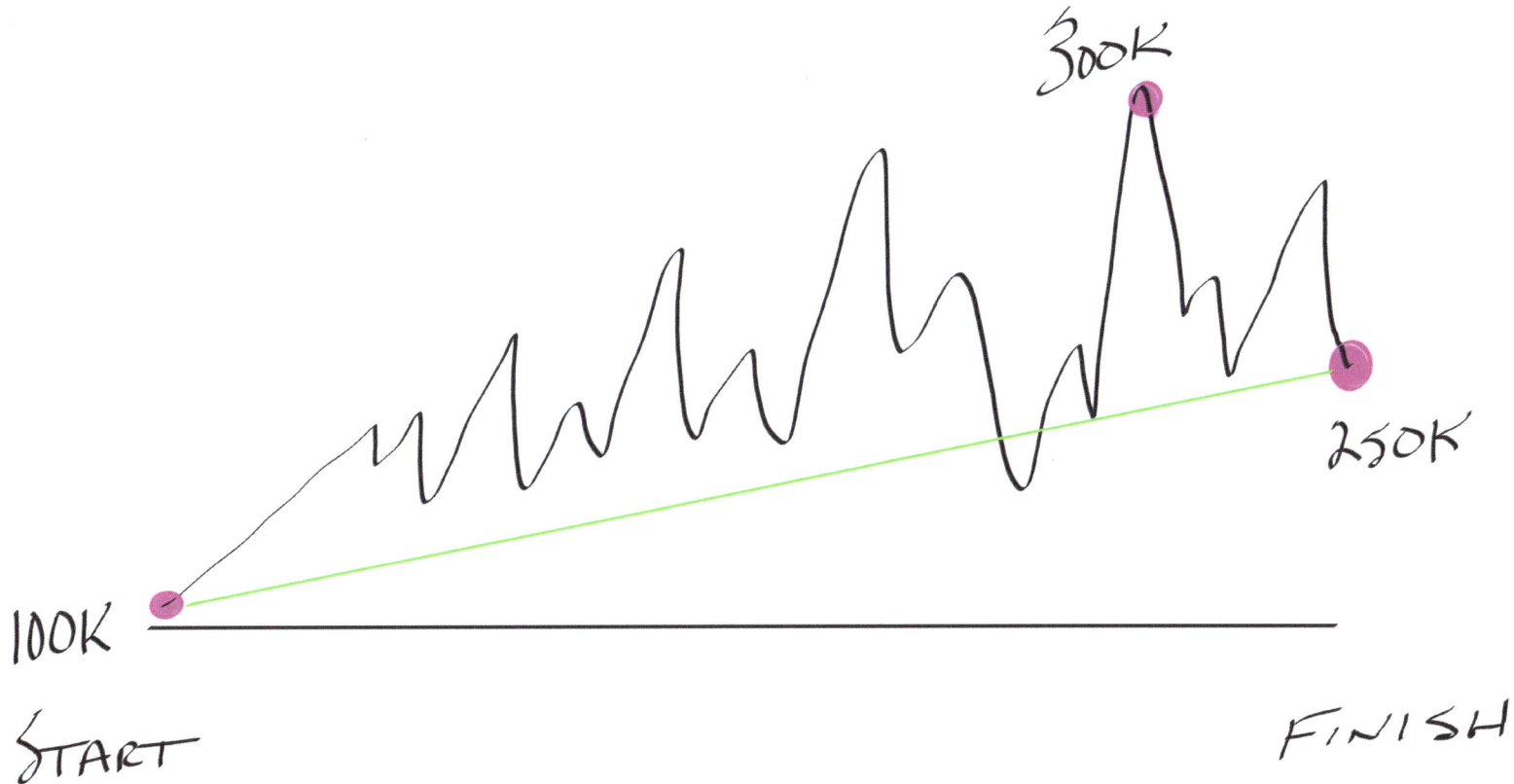

300K

250K

100K
START

FINISH

Nic

Do You Have An Income Protection Plan?

"A"	"B"
If HEALTHY...	If HEALTHY...
400K	392K
If DISABLED...	If DISABLED...
0	240K
Compensation	TAX FREE UNTIL AGE 65

Building Your Portfolio

① Asset Location

Taxable	Tax Deferred	Tax Free

② Asset Allocation

Stocks	Bonds	Cash	"Other"

③ Asset Selection

Individual Securities	ETF's	Mutual Funds	Annuities	Structured Products	"Other"

$\dfrac{N_{iL}^{\emptyset}}{\overline{\overline{e}}}$

Life Insurance Needs Analysis

Outstanding Debt	550K MTG
+	
Unfunded Liabilities	250K College
+	
Income Need ×12 / 4%	2.7m (9K × 12) / 4%
−	
Liquid Net Worth	(500K)
=	=
Insurance Needed	$3m

How To Own Stocks & Real Estate

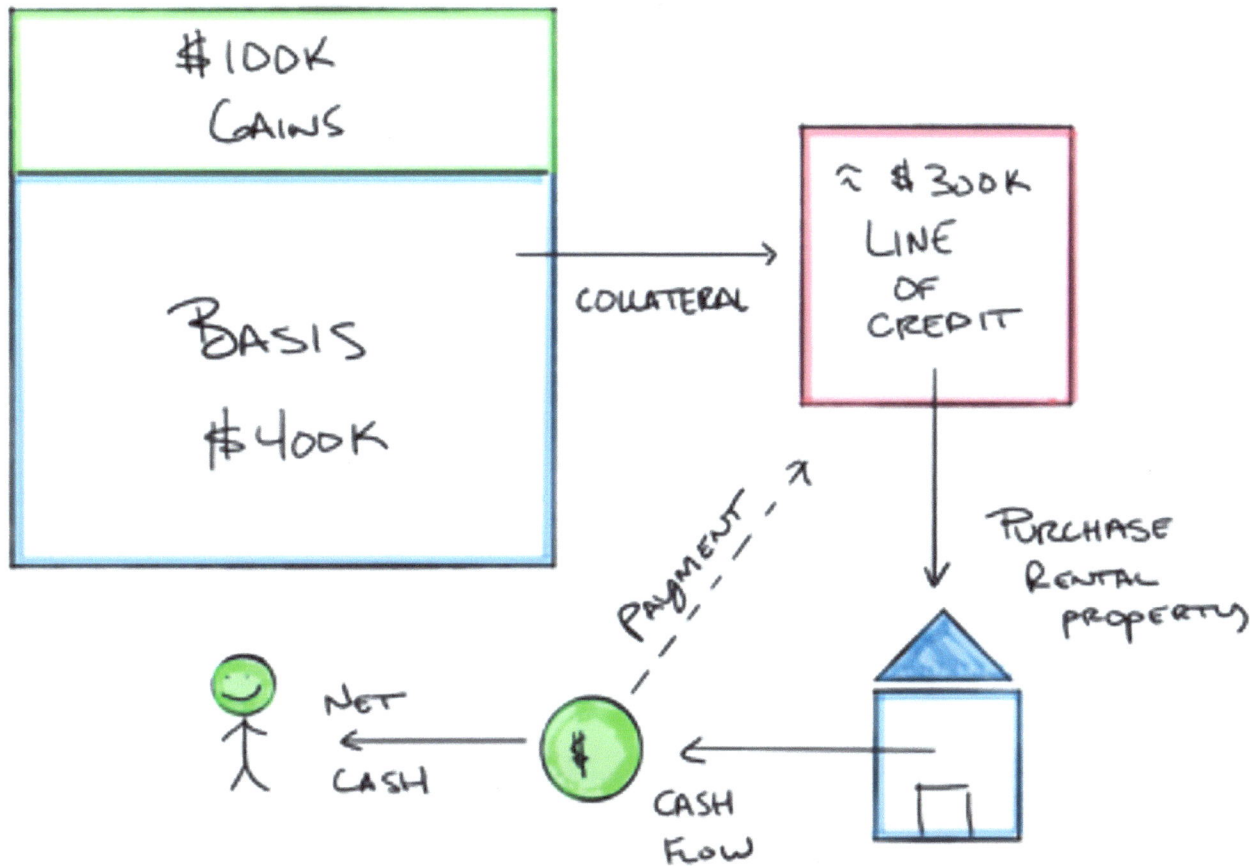

$100K
GAINS

BASIS
$400K

COLLATERAL →

≈ $300K
LINE
OF
CREDIT

PURCHASE
RENTAL
PROPERTY

PAYMENT

NET
CASH

CASH
FLOW

Nic

NET PAYCHECK

1 GIVE
- CHURCH
- CHARITY
- FRIENDS

NO $

2 AUTOMATED GOALS
- INVESTING
  - HSA
  - ROTH 401K
  - JOINT
- PROTECT
  - DISABILITY
  - LIFE

3 SPEND
- MORTGAGE
- STUDENT LOAN
- TRAVEL
- HOUSEHOLD NEEDS

THE PLANNING > THE PLAN

$\dfrac{N^{0}_{IC}}{\varepsilon}$

WHAT IS A ROTH?

"HARVEST"

③

GROWTH
0 TAX DEFERRED

②

"SEED"

①

DISTRIBUTIONS
0 TAX FREE

CONTRIBUTIONS
0 AFTER-TAX $

* PAY TAX ON THE SEED *
TO RECEIVE THE
HARVEST TAX FREE!

Nic

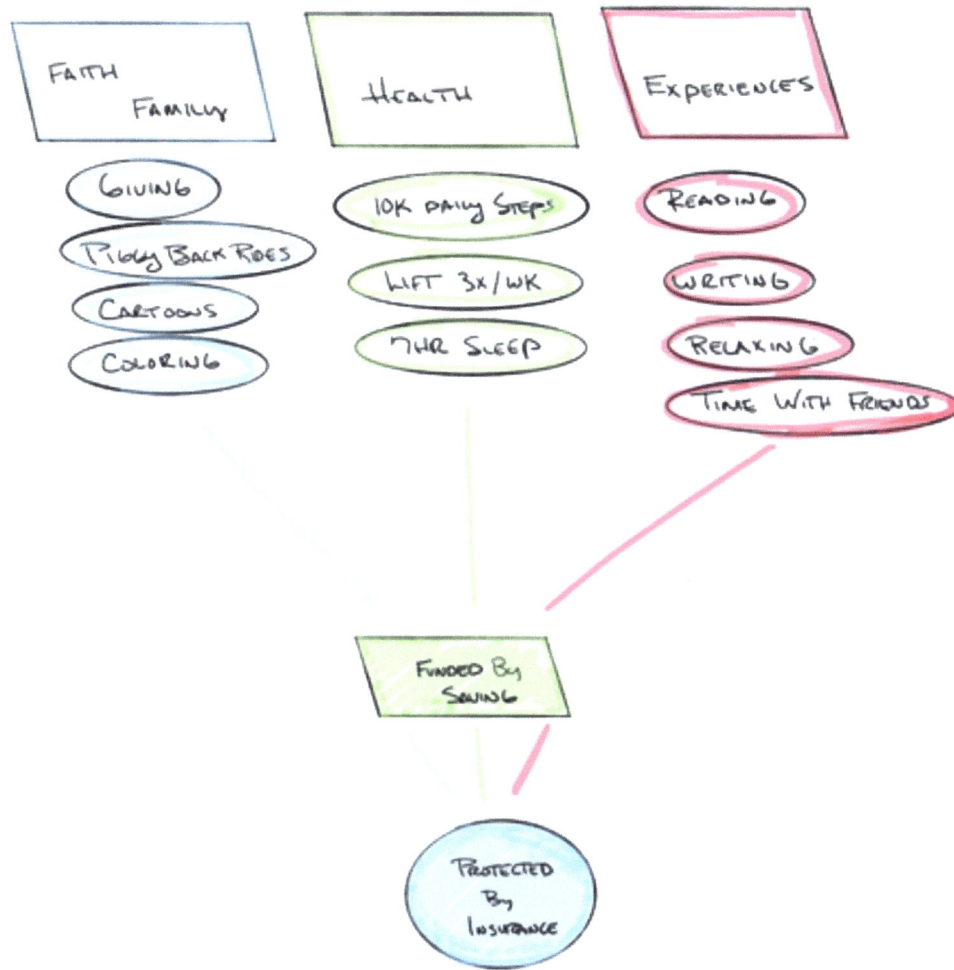

BEYOND CORE VALUES...

FAITH FAMILY
- GIVING
- PIGGY BACK RIDES
- CARTOONS
- COLORING

HEALTH
- 10K DAILY STEPS
- LIFT 3X/WK
- 7HR SLEEP

EXPERIENCES
- READING
- WRITING
- RELAXING
- TIME WITH FRIENDS

FUNDED BY SAVING

PROTECTED BY INSURANCE

Nic

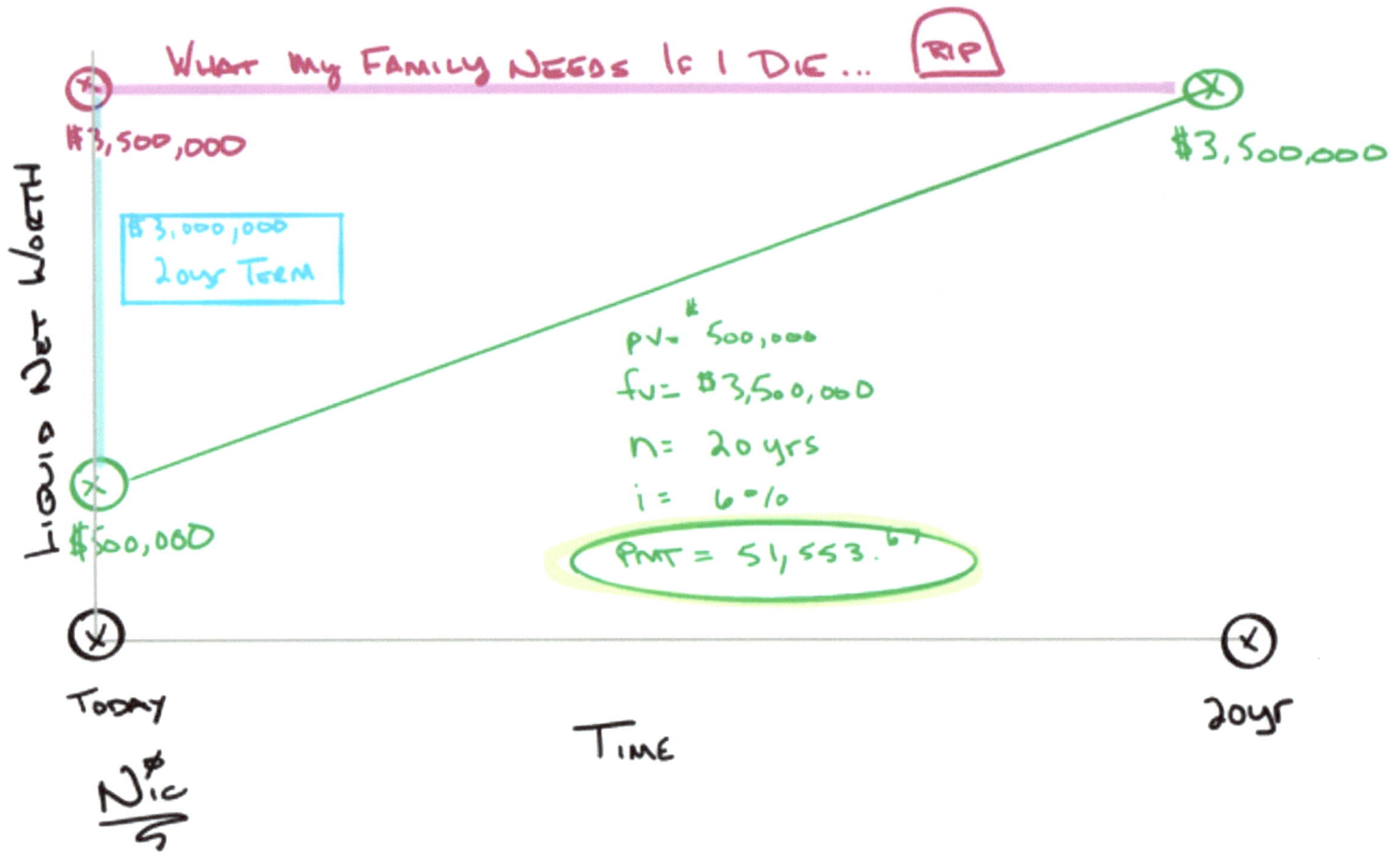

WHAT MY FAMILY NEEDS IF I DIE... RIP

$3,500,000

$3,000,000
20yr TERM

$3,500,000

LIQUID NET WORTH

pv = $500,000
fv = $3,500,000
n = 20 yrs
i = 6%
PMT = 51,553.⁶⁷

$500,000

TODAY

TIME

20yr

MANAGING YOUR TAX BRACKET

TAXABLE	TAX DEFERRED	TAX FREE

TYPE

• BROKERAGE	• 401K, 403B	• ROTH
• CHECKING	• IRA, SEP,	• HSA
• SAVINGS	SIMPLE	• CVLI • MUNI

GOAL

Small

Medium

BIG!

• EMERGENCY FUNDS

• STANDARD DEDUCTION OFFSET

• EVERYTHING ELSE!

Nic

"WHAT IS THE STOCK MARKET GOING TO DO?"

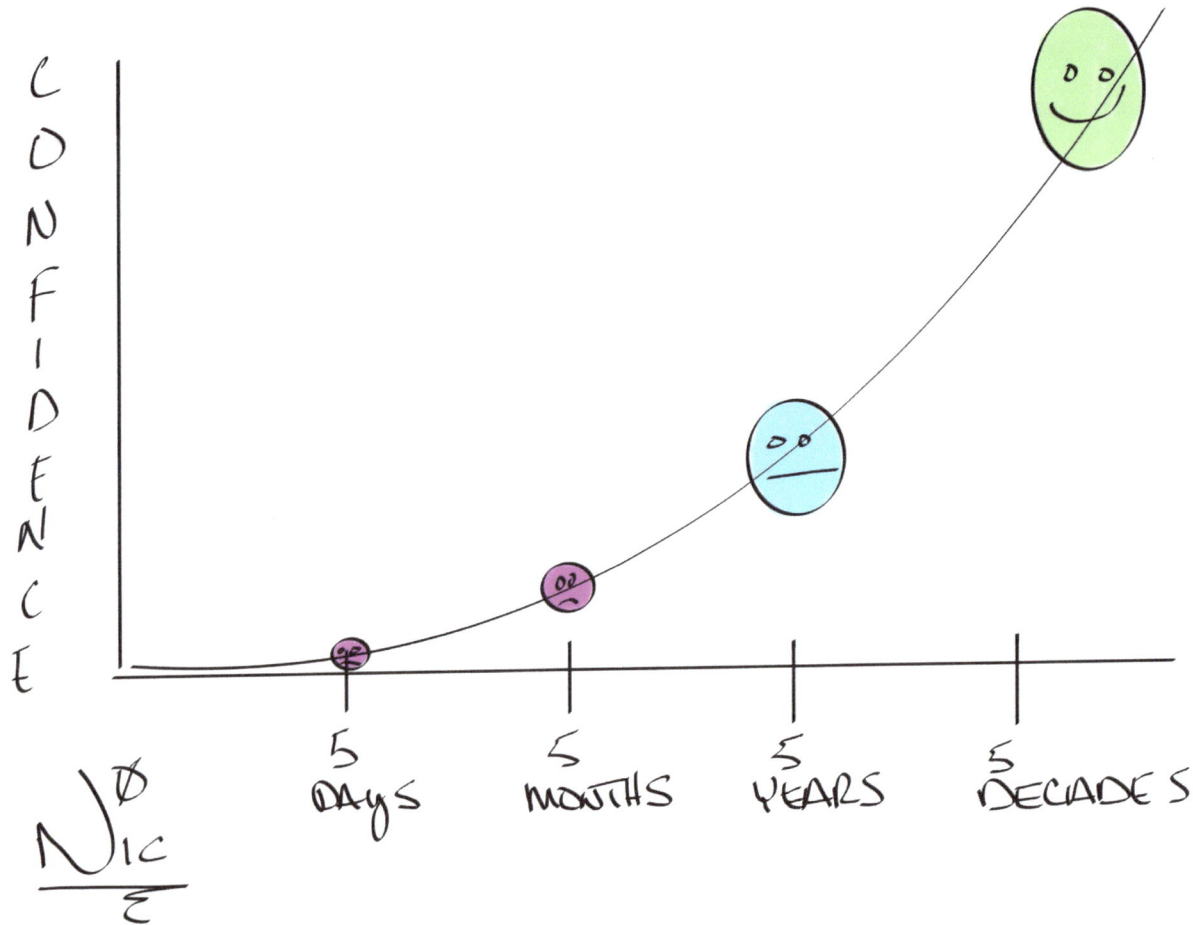

CONFIDENCE

NOT IC E

5 DAYS

5 MONTHS

5 YEARS

5 DECADES

SHOULD I CONSOLIDATE TO MY CURRENT 401K?

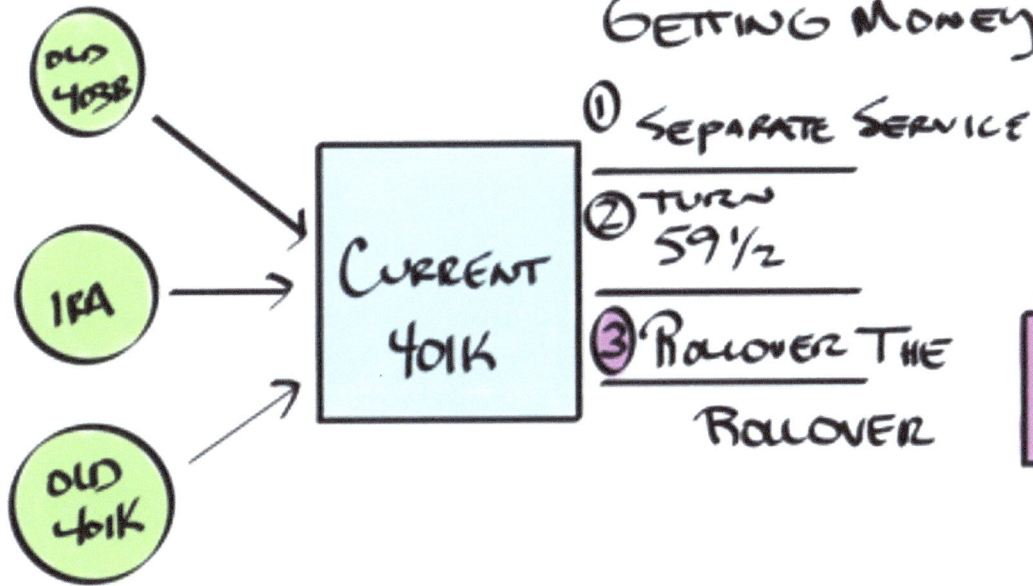

GETTING MONEY OUT...

① SEPARATE SERVICE

② TURN 59½

③ ROLLOVER THE ROLLOVER

→ NOTE:

YOU MIGHT NOT BE ABLE TO ROLL OUT WHAT YOU ROLLED IN UNLESS 1 OR 2 APPLY!

Nic

FILLING YOUR TAX BUCKET : ROTH CONVERSION

TAX RATES		
TAX RATE	MFJ	SINGLE
10%	$0 - $19,900	$0 - $9,950
12%	$19,900 - $81,050	$9,950 - $40,525
22%	$81,050 - $172,750	$40,525 - $86,375
24%	$172,750 - $329,850	$86,375 - $164,925
32%	$329,850 - $418,850	$164,925 - $209,425
35%	$418,850 - $628,300	$209,425 - $523,600
37%	Over $628,300	Over $523,600

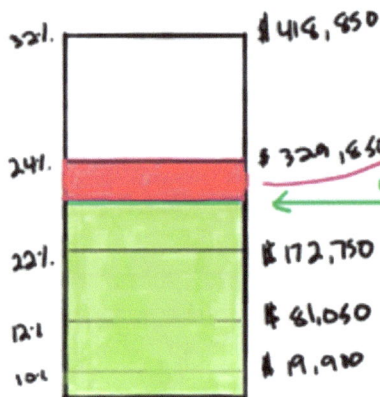

32% — $418,850

24% — $329,850

22% — $172,750

12% — $81,050

10% — $19,900

$250K SALARY

OPPORTUNITY
$329,850
- 250,000
_____
$79,850

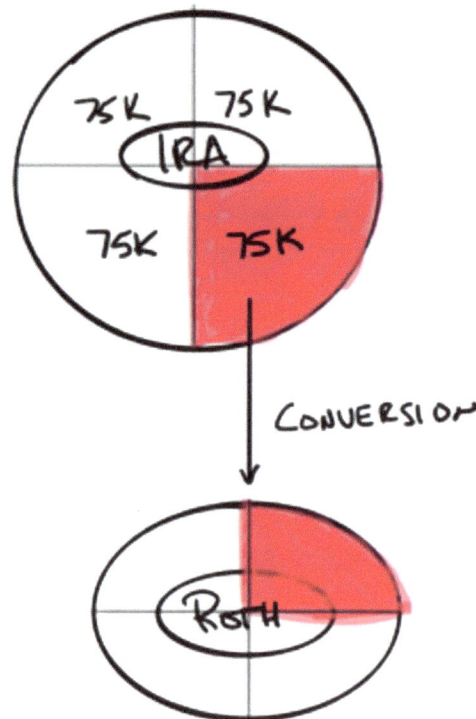

75K | 75K
IRA
75K | 75K

CONVERSION

Roth

Nic

CONTRIBUTING A HIGHER % COULD HURT YOU

SALARY	CONT 20%	MATCH 5%	or	CONT 10%	MATCH 5%
195K					
16,250	3,250	812.50		1,625	812.50
16,250	3,250	812.50		1,625	812.50
16,250	3,250	812.50		1,625	812.50
16,250	3,250	812.50		1,625	812.50
16,250	3,250	812.50		1,625	812.50
16,250	3,250	812.50		1,625	812.50
16,250				1,625	812.50
16,250				1,625	812.50
16,250				1,625	812.50
16,250				1,625	812.50
16,250				1,625	812.50
16,250				1,625	812.50
TOTAL	19,500	4,875		19,500	9,750

Nic

PREPARE FOR THE DIP: ROTH CONVERSION

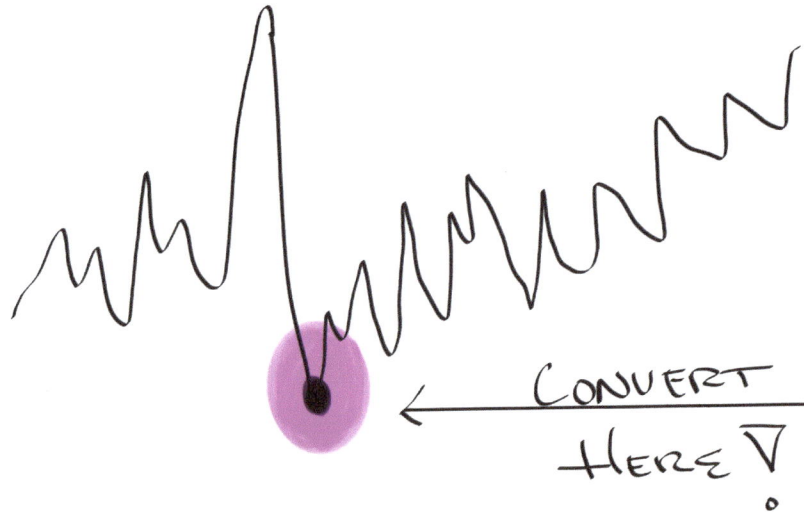

CONVERT HERE ∇

PREPARE DON'T PREDICT!

I JUST HEARD
IN THE NEWS,

I SHOULD ...

[INSERT Apocalypse du Jour]

FOR YOUR Portfolio

Nic

BLUE CHIPS
SMALL CAP
EMERGING MARKET
REAL ESTATE
CORE BOND
GOLD
CURRENCY

AVOID THE SMARTEST WIZARD !

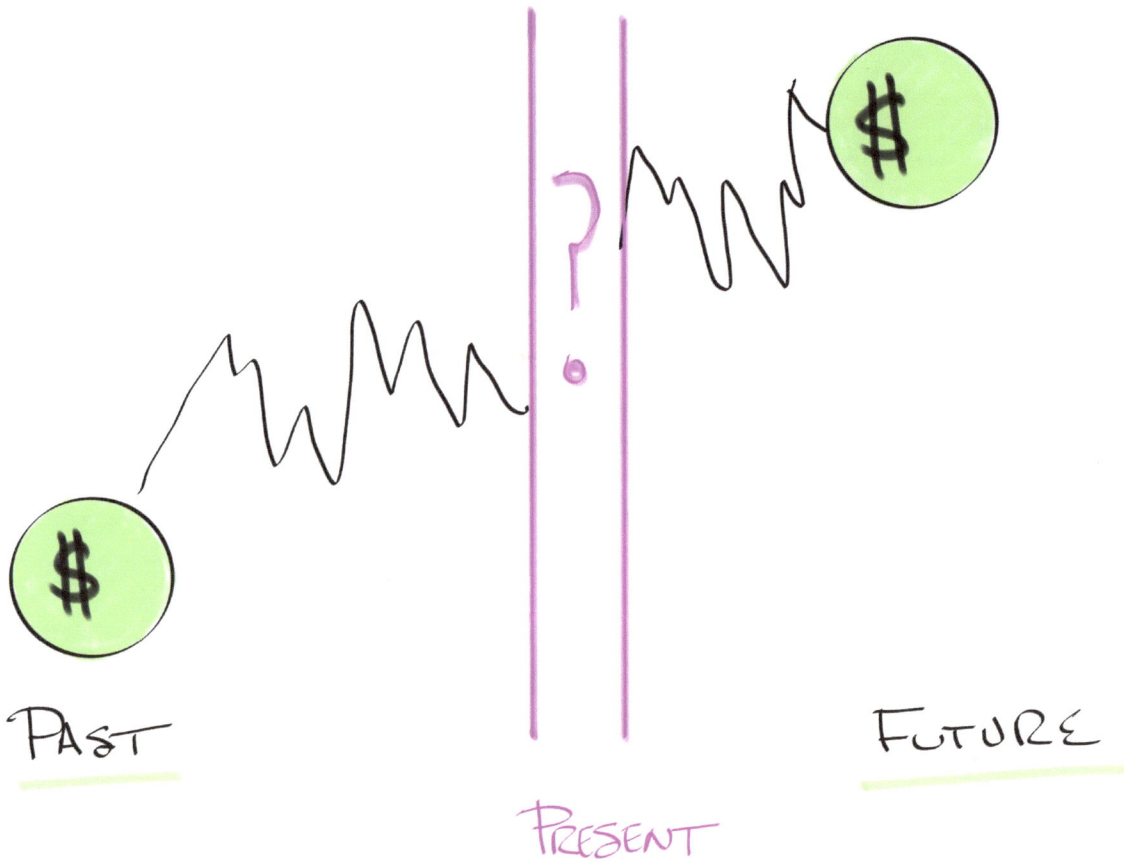

PAST

PRESENT

FUTURE

BUILDING YOUR ASSET ALLOCATION

Why?
1 LIQUIDITY
2 SAFETY

Why?
1 "SAFER" FIXED INCOME IS NEEDED WHEN "GROWTH" IS ↓
2 ↑ RETURN THAN "CASH"

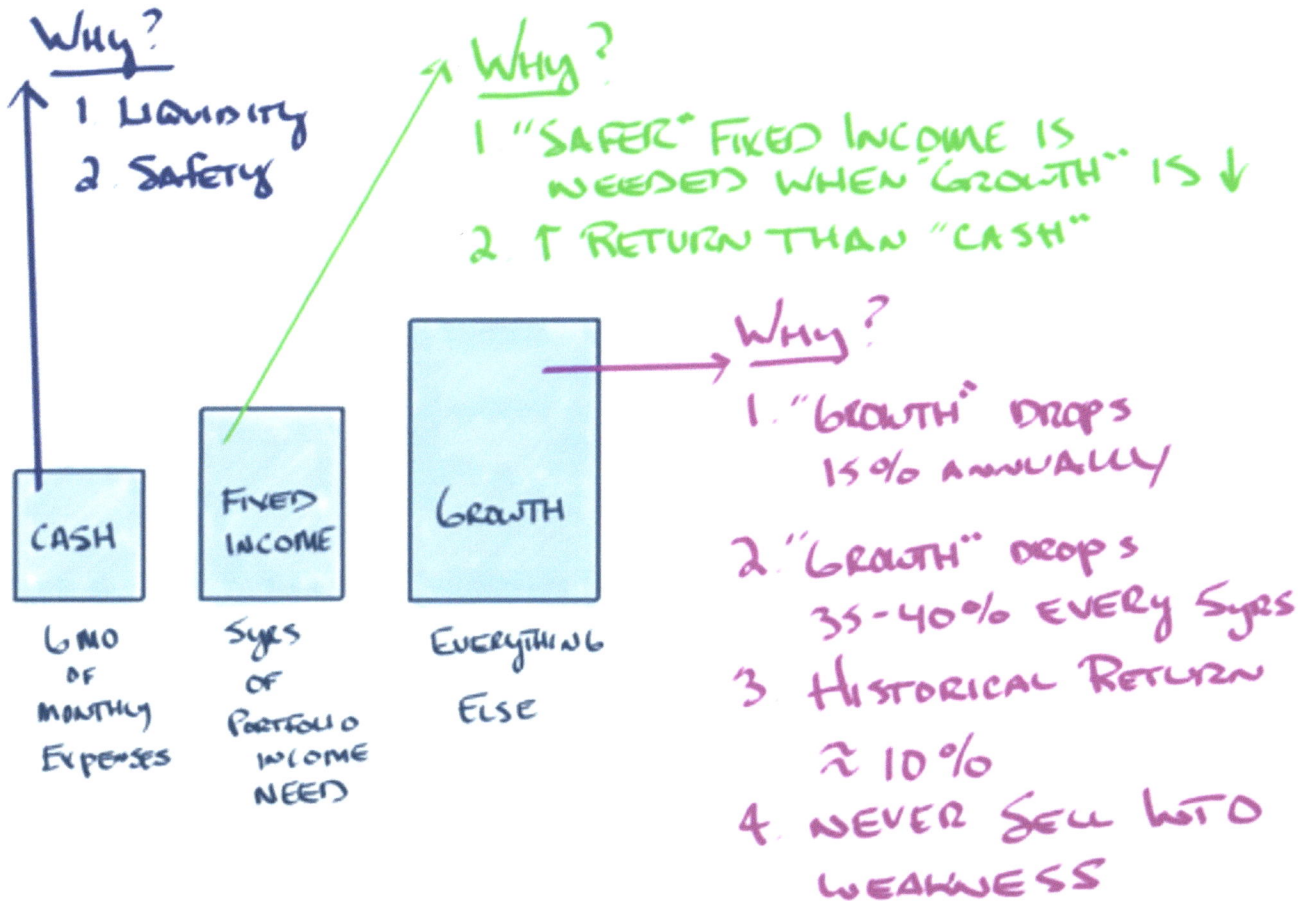

CASH
6 MO
OF
MONTHLY
EXPENSES

FIXED INCOME
5 YRS
OF
PORTFOLIO
INCOME
NEED

GROWTH
EVERYTHING
ELSE

Why?
1. "GROWTH" DROPS 15% ANNUALLY
2. "GROWTH" DROPS 35-40% EVERY 5 YRS
3 HISTORICAL RETURN ≈ 10%
4 NEVER SELL INTO WEAKNESS

Nic

If I Could Invest Anywhere...

1. Health Savings Account

2. Roth IRA / 401K / 403B

3. After - Tax 401K / 403B

4A. Individual Account w/ Line Of Credit

4B. Cash Value Life Insurance

6. Pre - Tax IRA / 401K

Nic

BENEFICIARY DESIGNATION

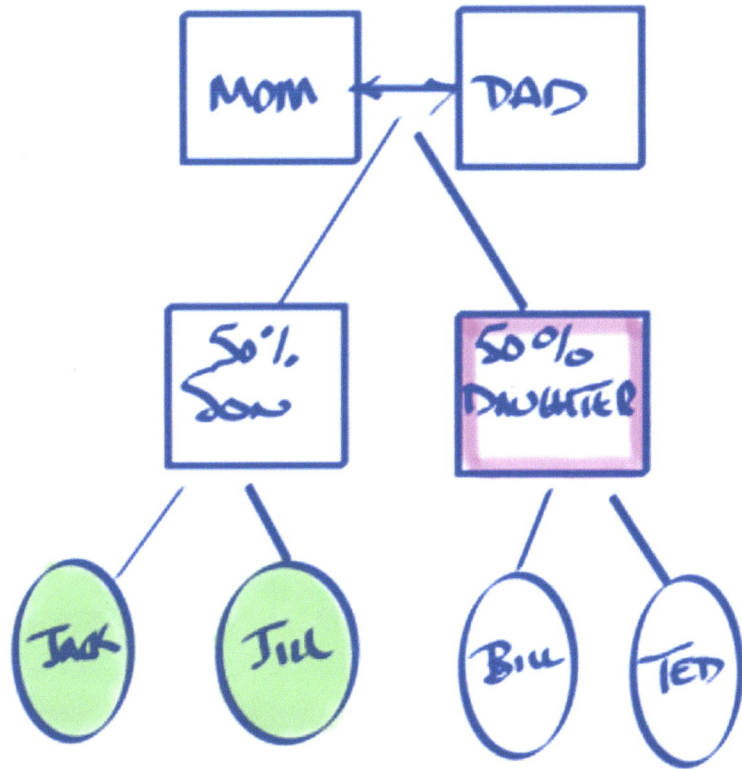

* WHAT HAPPENS IF THE SON DIES BEFORE HIS PARENTS?

→ PER CAPITA
   100% → DAUGHTER

→ PER STIRPES

   THE SON'S CHILDREN WOULD RECEIVE THE FUNDS (50%)

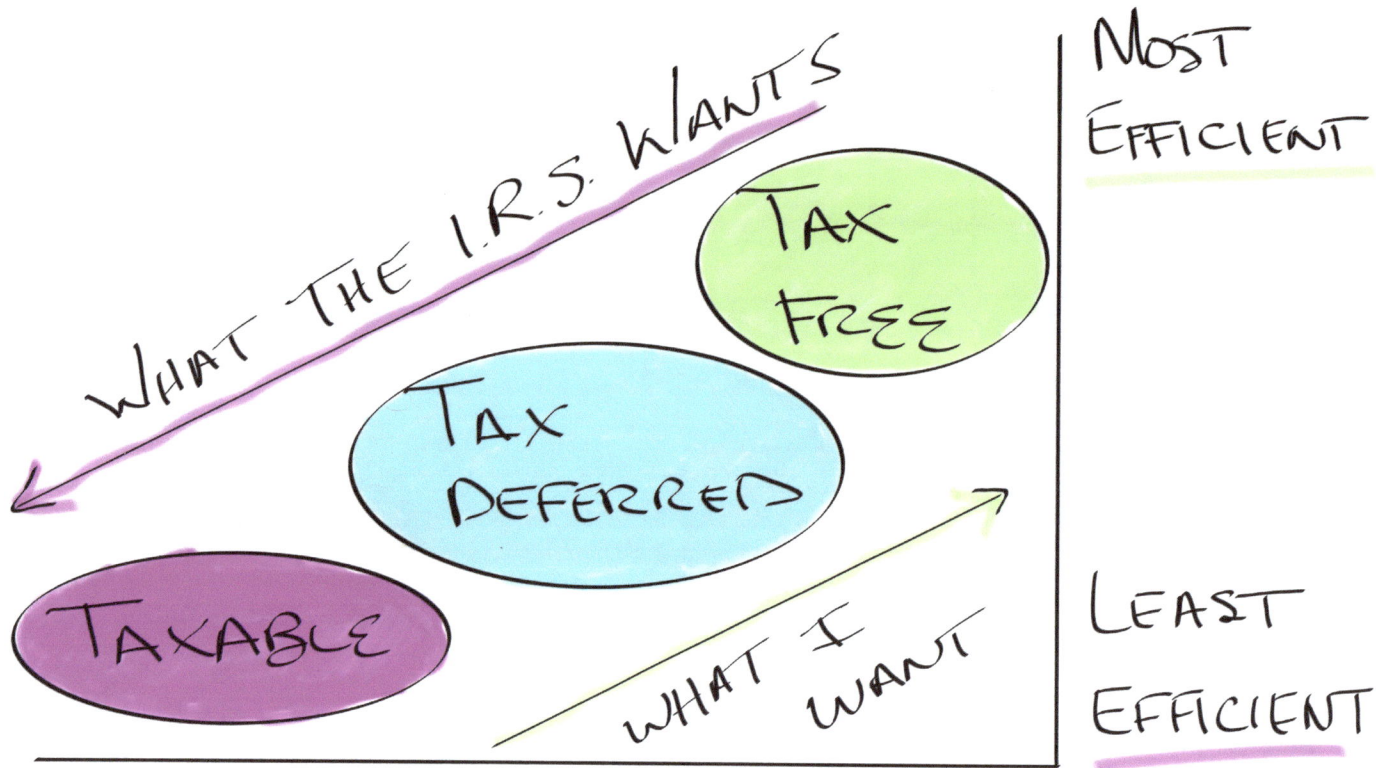

WHAT THE I.R.S. WANTS

MOST
EFFICIENT

TAX
FREE

TAX
DEFERRED

TAXABLE

WHAT I WANT

LEAST
EFFICIENT

Nⁱᶜ

Getting Outside The Stock Market Blast Zone

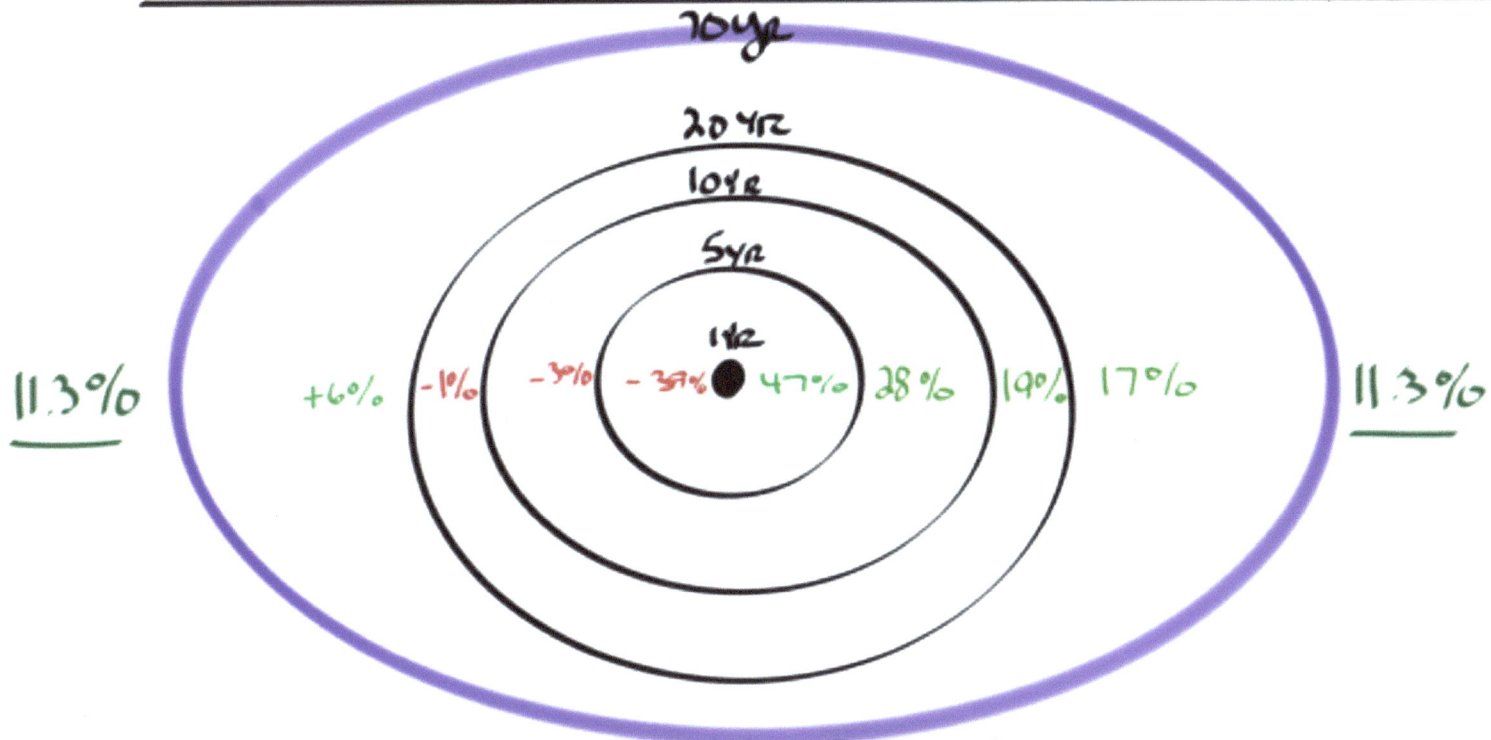

11.3% — +6% -1% -3% -37% 47% 28% 19% 17% — 11.3%

20yr
20yr
10yr
5yr
1yr

WORST CASE · BEST CASE

1950 - 2020
S&P 500
ROLLING PERIODS

$\frac{N^o_{ic}}{\Sigma}$

T.A.G. YOUR SAVINGS

① Tax Efficient

BEFORE SAVING

③ Growth

② Access

THE METAMORPHOSIS OF A GROWTH SECURITY

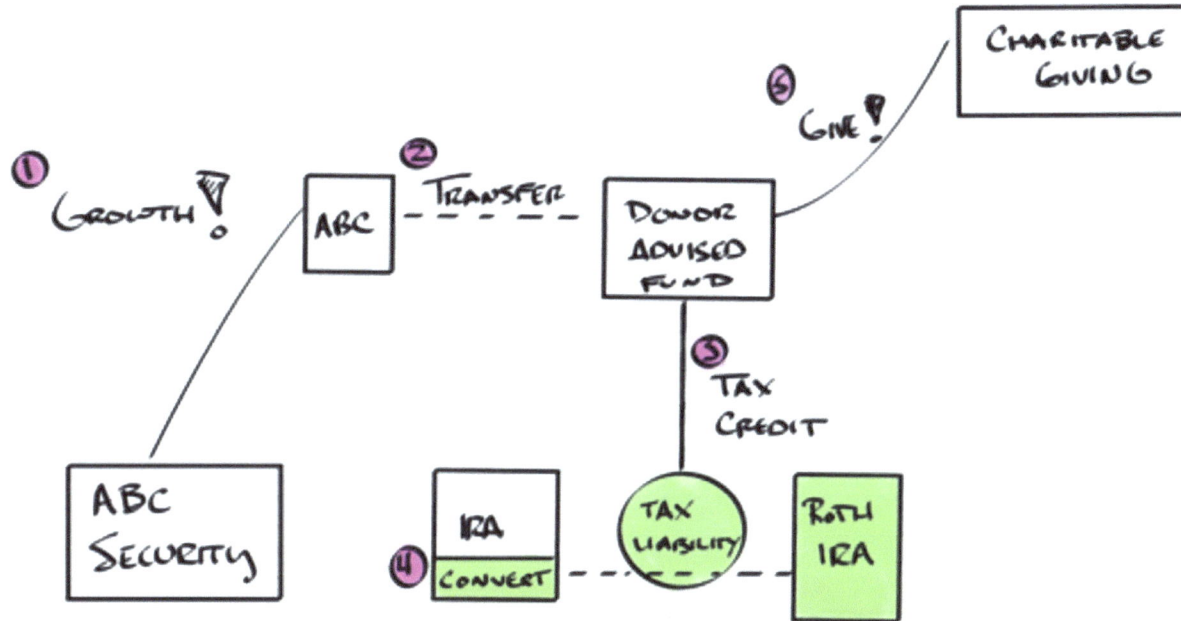

NIc

UNDERSTANDING THE "LINE IN THE SAND"

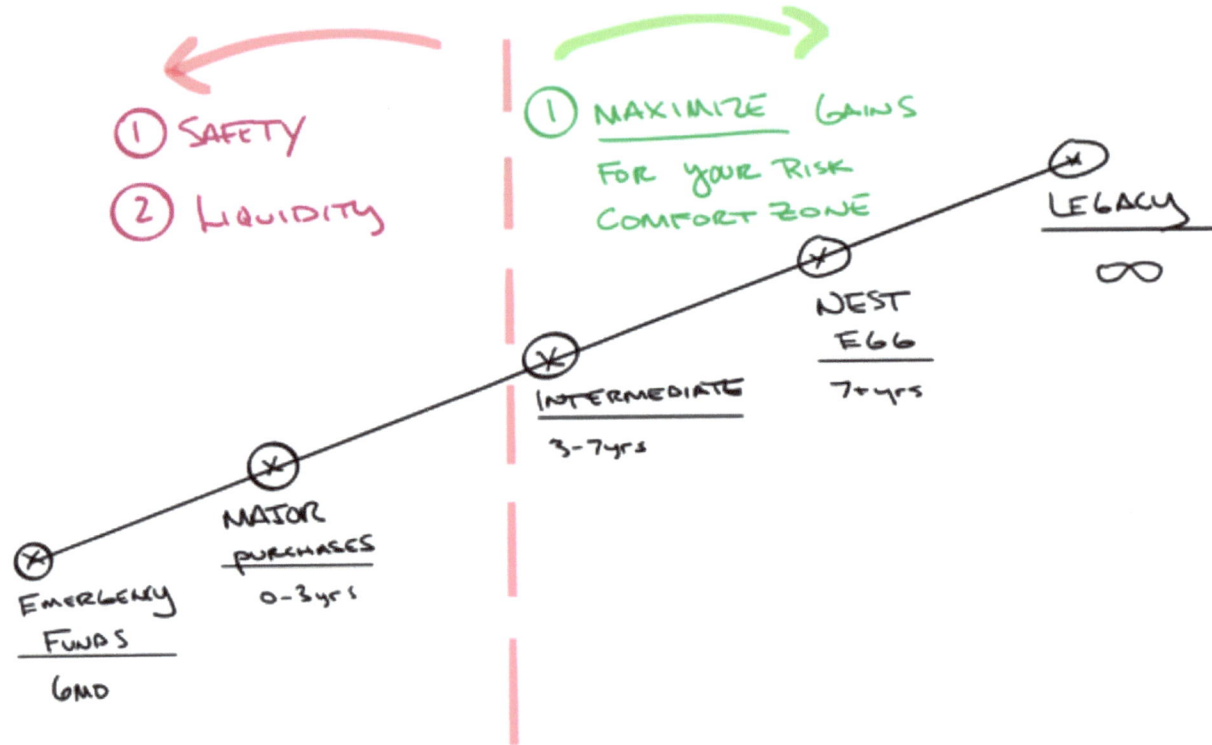

① SAFETY

② LIQUIDITY

① MAXIMIZE GAINS FOR YOUR RISK COMFORT ZONE

EMERGENCY FUNDS
6MO

MAJOR PURCHASES
0-3yrs

INTERMEDIATE
3-7yrs

NEST EGG
7+yrs

LEGACY
∞

Nic
?

How Much Does Your Car Really Cost?

Depreciation	Appreciation
	STOCKS BONDS CASH
CAR PAYMENT	BALANCED FUND
$600/MONTH	$600/MONTH
20 YEARS	20 YEARS
($144,000)	$277,224 ⓐ 6%

Nic

WANTS VS. NEEDS

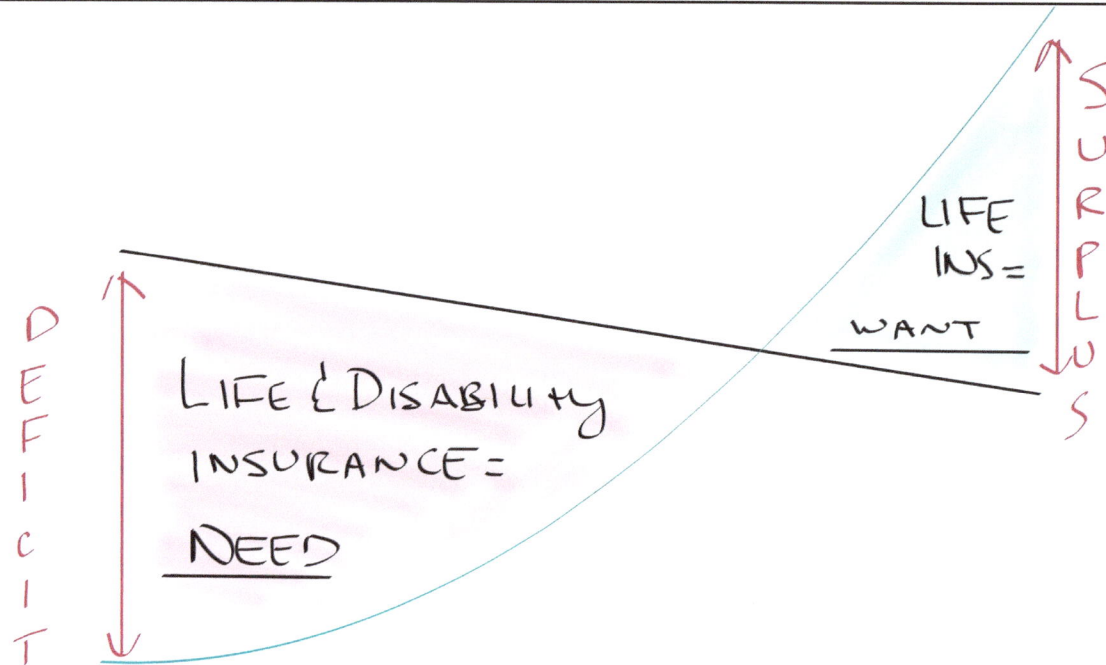

LIFE INS = WANT

SURPLUS

DEFICIT

LIFE & DISABILITY INSURANCE = NEED

■ ASSETS NEEDED IF I DIE

■ ASSETS

$$\frac{N\phi_c}{S}$$

Reframing "Risk"

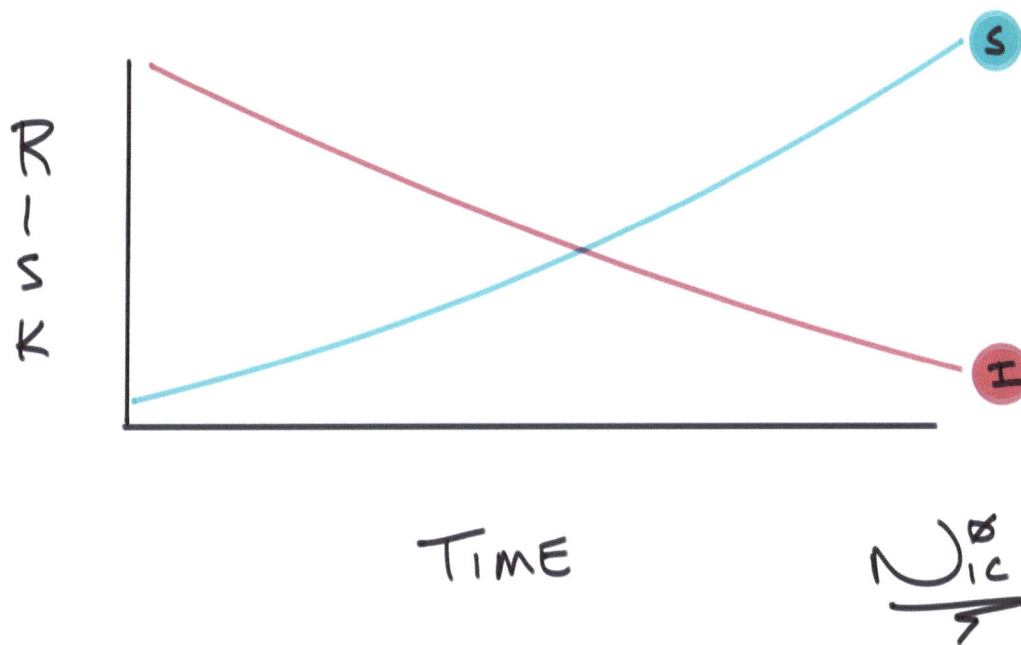

S "Save"

I "Invest"

* 40-Year *
Scorecard

1. S&P 500

    1982 117.30

    2021 4,766

    40x

2. Dividends Per Share

    1982 $19.62

    2021 $60.40

    2.08x

3. Inflation

    1982 94.30

    2021 279

    1.96x

www.knowmyplan.com